Incredibly Insane Sports

MOUNTAIN CLIMBING

By Jessica Cohn

Gareth Stevens
Publishing

Please visit our website, www.garethstevens.com. For a free color catalog of all our high-quality books, call toll free 1-800-542-2595 or fax 1-877-542-2596.

Library of Congress Cataloging-in-Publication Data

Cohn, Jessica.
 Mountain clmbing / Jessica Cohn.
      p. cm. — (Incredibly insane sports)
 Includes index.
ISBN 978-1-4339-8831-8 (pbk.)
ISBN 978-1-4339-8832-5 (6-pack)
ISBN 978-1-4339-8830-1 (library binding)
1. Mountaineering--Juvenile literature. I. Title.
GV200.C63 2013
 796.522—dc23
                              2012037837

First Edition
Published in 2013 by
Gareth Stevens Publishing
111 East 14th Street, Suite 349
New York, NY 10003

©2013 Gareth Stevens Publishing

Produced by Netscribes Inc.
Art Director Dibakar Acharjee
Editorial Content The Wordbench
Copy Editor Sarah Chassé
Picture Researcher Sandeep Kumar G
Designer Rishi Raj
Illustrators Ashish Tanwar, Indranil Ganguly, Prithwiraj Samat and Rohit Sharma

Photo credits:

Page no. = #, t = top, a = above, b = below, l = left, r = right, c = center
Front Cover: Shutterstock Images LLC Title Page: Shutterstock Images LLC
Contents Page: Shutterstock Images LLC Inside: Netscribes Inc.: 9bl Shutterstock Images LLC: 4, 5t, 5bl, 5br, 6, 7t, 7b, 8t, 8b, 9t, 9br, 10, 11, 12t, 12b, 13t, 13c, 13b, 14, 15, 16, 17, 18, 19t, 19b, 20, 21t, 21b, 22, 23, 24, 25, 26, 27, 28, 29, 30, 31, 32, 33t, 33b, 34, 35, 36, 37, 38, 39t, 39b, 40, 41, 42, 43.

Printed in the United States of America

CPSIA compliance information: Batch #CW13GS: For further information contact Gareth Stevens, New York, New York at 1-800-542-2595.

Contents

PEAK EXPERIENCE

For pure danger, it is hard to beat K2, which is the second-tallest mountain in the world. Climbing this peak is one of the most difficult adventures anyone can undertake. The mountaintop is protected by huge ice pillars. The ice stands like a great fence or wall. It seems to block those who dare to climb so close to the clouds.

The top of K2 was reached for the first time in 1954. The mountain's deadliest year was 1986, when 27 people climbed it and 13 died.

Extreme Heights

People who reach for the highest peaks are extreme athletes. Each mountain presents tall challenges for its climbers to overcome. On the world's tallest mountains, the air is thin, and the weather can be wild. The sheer isolation makes many mountains dangerous, because there is no one there to help if the climbers fall.

Rock-craft is the skill needed to climb on rock. Ice-craft is needed to climb sheets of ice. There is also a set of skills known as snow-craft.

Goal Getters

The "eight-thousanders" are the 14 mountains that stand higher than 26,247 feet above sea level, or 8,000 meters tall. The first person to climb all 14 accomplished this feat in 1986. Since then, about 30 people have completed the list.

The Seven Summits are the tallest mountains on all seven continents. The first person to climb all of them did so in 1985. To date, there have been over 100 people who claim to have reached the top of all seven.

Some people say they climb mountains for fun. For other people, it is a way to make a living. They live near mountains and work as guides for the climbers.

6

Living Danger

Mountain climbing is also called mountaineering, and the people who participate are known as mountaineers. In rock climbing, the mountaineers attempt to scale rocks. In ice climbing, the challenge is to climb huge blocks of frozen ground and ice. When climbing on rock, there is more friction holding the climber in place. But both kinds of mountaineering are dangerous.

When climbing a wall, you can feel the friction in the heat on your hands.

TEST IT!

When two things rub together, the rough edges of one will rub the rough edges of the other, and they will both slow down. This is because of the force called friction. If you pay attention to the world around you, you will notice that there is more friction between solid things. If one thing is solid and the other is liquid, there is less friction. It is easier for the solid material to slip.

7

CLIMB EVERY MOUNTAIN

Earth has a mind-blowing variety of mountains to explore. In North America, the highest peaks include mountains in Alaska and Wyoming and summits in the Pacific Northwest and in the Southwest. There are a dozen mountains in California that climbers consider world-class mountains.

Devils Tower, in Wyoming, is covered with wide cracks that make it a special challenge. Climbers must register with the National Park Service before going to the top.

Alaska has 14 major mountain ranges to explore. Adventure clubs and schools have been established to teach climbing skills to visitors.

Park It

Joshua Tree National Park is about three hours east of Los Angeles, California. Climbers call the park J-Tree. It is famous for bouldering, which is climbing rocks that are relatively small, compared with mountains. Within J-Tree, there are more than 8,000 climbing routes. Most of them are less than 100 feet high. Both beginners and advanced climbers find something to enjoy, especially since the park can be warm and sunny in winter.

TEST IT!

How do you measure the **slope** of a mountain? Imagine a line going straight up the mountain's side. Then, imagine a line across its base, which meets the other line.

To measure the angles for yourself, use thin paper and a sharp pencil. Trace this protractor, which is a tool for measuring angles. Line up the "nose" of each angle with the red dot on the tool.

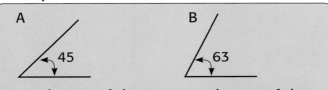

A   45   B   63

A: 45 degrees of slope   B: 63 degrees of slope

Onward

Throughout history, people have been attempting to reach mountaintops or cross mountain ranges. But today's climbers have an edge over the climbers of long ago. Modern climbers benefit from climbing innovations. For example, new materials with better grip have been put into the shoes. In addition, today's climbers have an easier time finding places where they can practice. Many gyms are set up to help people train for mountaineering. New climbers can work on their footing on rock walls built for indoor practice. They can work on their **back steps** while being coached.

Upward

Beginning climbers tend to try to lift themselves by the arms. This kind of movement places a lot of pressure on the arms and hands, so it is common for people to injure fingers at the start. People who are new to climbing must learn to push up from the legs and use the forward movement to their advantage. To master the moves, it is necessary to put in time learning the **techniques**. Like most things that people must practice, it takes thousands of hours to become an expert.

To climb faster, people learn to climb smarter. They look for effective moves and try to find a pace that works for them.

11

HISTORY'S PEAKS

People have been climbing mountains since ancient times, but long ago, people climbed only as needed. Early people climbed mountain ranges to hunt animals, settle in new areas, or fight wars with people from other lands. This has changed in recent years, when climbing has been done more as a sport and a challenge.

Edmund Hillary, of New Zealand, and Tenzing Norgay, of Nepal, were the first to reach the top of Mount Everest.

Climbs and Times

1868   Climbers reached the top of the tallest mountain in Europe, Mount Elbrus.

1889   Climbers first reached the top of Kilimanjaro, in Africa.

1897   Mountaineers made it to the top of Aconcagua, in South America.

1913   Climbers scaled Mount McKinley, the highest North American mountain.

1953   Climbers reach the summit of Mount Everest, the tallest mountain in Asia and the world.

Mount Elbrus

Aconcagua

The tallest peak in North America is in Alaska. It was called Mount McKinley by outsiders who traveled to it when William McKinley was president. Native Alaskans call it Denali, which means "the great one" in the early languages used in the area.

13

Path to the Top

In mountaineering, there is a way up and a way down. But there are no two ways about the danger involved. Mountain climbing is a sport filled with risks, and the most effective way to cut those risks is to train well. Besides practicing the skills needed, it is important to make a plan. Successful climbers gain as much knowledge as possible about what the weather will be like. They study the path to take and pack items that can be helpful if there are problems.

One of the first rules of climbing is to inspect all the equipment before going out.

Plan for Safety

Natural **hazards** are a natural part of outdoor climbs. Before any climb, the climbers check with people who have gone before them. They research the land and learn about the resources and help that are available in communities near the mountain. Experienced climbers make a formal safety plan. The plan includes the way up, the way down, and what can be done in case of an emergency.

People who climb in teams agree beforehand on the simple calls they will use to tell one another what has to be done next.

KNOWING THE ROPES

When a mountaineer uses special gear, such as ropes and picks, it is called aided climbing. When the climber uses hands and feet to get to the top, it is called free climbing. A free climber has less to pack than an aided climber—and can attempt some climbs alone. Aided climbers more often need to have help and work as part of a team.

Pick of Equipment

To travel on ice, a mountaineer packs an ice ax, which can be used as a walking stick when the land is flat. As the climber goes higher, and the mountainside turns into a slide, the ax can be used as a pick. It can help support the climber's weight on the way to the top. To walk on snow and ice, mountaineers wear **crampons**. This gear is strapped to the bottom of the climbers' boots. Crampons have long spikes that dig into snow and ice to keep people from slipping.

A climber's equipment includes rope and carabiners. Those are metal loops that spring open and shut.

Rope Trick

Climbers often tie rope to a harness that they wear. They toss the rope up around something secure, such as the point of a rock. In some cases, the climbers use bolts that were driven into the rock by people who came before them. Often, the rope then runs down to a **belayer**, who stands below. This is a person who adjusts the rope during the climb. The rope is threaded through a metal loop that keeps the rope from getting caught. The belayer feeds the rope as needed and pulls it tight when needed.

Material World

Climbing equipment performs some basic functions, such as helping the climber stay balanced. But the tools are anything but basic. Advances in materials have resulted in lighter, more dependable clinbing gear. The newest backpacks barely weigh anything, yet they can carry a huge load of supplies. The newest kinds of ropes last longer than ever.

The harness is attached to several points on the body. That way the feeling of force and stress caused by the climb are spread out across the body.

Gear Up

In days past, crampons were made from steel, and they were heavy for their size. Today, they are made of metals that can be 50 percent lighter. The lighter metals are being used for all kinds of climbing tools, such as axes. The materials for the equipment keep getting lighter and stronger.

The handholds on climbing walls are closely spaced so people of many sizes can climb successfully.

TEST IT!

Tension is the pulling force found in a rope that is attached to a climber. The weight of the climber is supported by the rope. When there is more than one anchor at the top of the rope, the tension is shared by each one. The more anchors there are, the less tension is released if one breaks. This means the climber will be jerked around less.

Sure-Footed

What mountaineers wear can make a difference in their performance. Beginning climbers often start by wearing gym shoes or boots. But special climbing shoes that fit close to the foot can help climbers advance their skills. To do serious mountain climbing, the athletes must pack clothes that can be worn in layers. Most people prefer items made of materials that let air in and sweat out.

Rock shoes have a special shape and hard bottom to make the climb easier.

Cold Facts

When climbing in ice and snow, it's not enough to pack mittens for sleeping. Climbers also bring mitten liners to keep their hands warm. The climbers also have to think of what they might need if things go wrong. They pack **thermal** leggings and undershirts. They also bring items such as extra socks and plastic foot liners.

Crampons have as many as 14 points to dig into the ice.

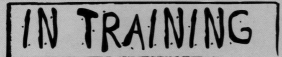

IN TRAINING

I n many sports, athletes perform better by practicing the moves they will use at a big event. But it is not possible to practice climbing each day leading to a big climb. The athletes must also do other kinds of exercise.

Why Weight?

Lifting weights builds strength. But simple muscle strength is not the kind that helps the most with climbing. The climber's endurance, or the ability to last with the heart pumping fast, is more important. Climbers must also be ready to perform upward movements. This means they must train muscles to move in a wide **range**, such as doing squats and exercises in which the legs switch back and forth.

Just Breathe

High in the mountains, the air is thin. There is less air pressure around the climber at those heights, which means less air and oxygen. So the heart has to pump faster. To prepare for time spent at high **altitudes**, many climbers go through special training. They concentrate on running and cycling to help build up the strength of their lungs and hearts.

Biking helps with leg movement and with the ability to stay alert while moving. Both are important skills for climbers to practice.

Uphill Battle

In the months before a major climb, the athletes work out more days than they rest. They build their ability to stay in action for long periods of time. Trainers encourage the athletes to push for extra effort at the end of their workouts. In this way, they are prepared for the times when they need to push themselves while on a climb.

The lower body works the hardest while climbing, so it is important to build lower body strength. Climbing stairs and hiking both build this strength.

Daily Diet

Climbing involves long days of exercise. It is important to eat a balanced diet and to stay **hydrated**. When movement is constant, the body needs food from which it can quickly take energy. This means eating plenty of **carbohydrates**, such as oatmeal. Many climbers rely on something called GORP. That stands for "Good Old Raisins and Peanuts."

Climbers avoid foods with simple sugars. These foods can lead to an energy crash.

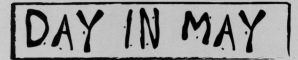

DAY IN MAY

A major climb takes major planning. The people who climb Mount Everest apply for permits months ahead of time. Many go to the mountain in May, when the weather is the best. Even then, it is very cold at the top. They have to collect a long list of equipment to deal with the extreme weather.

The weather for climbing Everest is best in May because the average speed of the wind slows down then.

First Stop

A trip to Mount Everest costs thousands of dollars. The would-be climbers must fly to Kathmandu. This is a town in Nepal, which is in Asia. There, the mountaineers need to organize a group to go with them.

Top It Off

A team that climbs the South Col climbs 17,500 feet (5,334 m) just to get to the **base camp**. There, they rest and try to get used to the thin air. Then, they try to scale the ice. They rest again at Camp 1, then they climb to Camp 2 and Camp 3. Each climb is thousands of feet long. When they reach 26,300 feet (8,016 m), they are at Camp 4 and an area of the mountain called the Death Zone. There, the climbers wait and hope for weather that will allow them to go to the very top.

What Do You Think?

Climbers tend to be people who enjoy nature and the great outdoors. They speak of their duty to leave little or no mark on the land. Do you think this is important? Why or why not?

The South Col is one of several paths that lead up Mount Everest. Each path includes areas where the climbers rest.

NO CONTEST

Most climbers compete only with themselves, meeting special challenges they have set as goals. But climbing competitions have been growing in popularity. Most of these events take place on artificial rock walls. The first major world event of this kind was held in 1985, and the sport has been getting bigger ever since.

Know the Score

Lead competitions are contests with three rounds. These are known as the **qualifications**, the semifinals, and the finals. In the first round, the climbers often follow routes that they were allowed to study. Then, they are ranked by how well they performed. In the next round, the climbers do not see the route until several minutes ahead of time. The finals, or third round, determine the winners. If there is a tie, the time it took each climber to complete the climb is also compared.

Fast and Furious

Some contests are totally based on speed, and the climbers compete in timed contests. The racers perform several times, and each time they get scores. In the end, they are compared with all the people in the same class. The more points, the more likely it is that individuals and teams will advance.

Olympic officials are considering adding sports climbing to the 2020 Olympics.

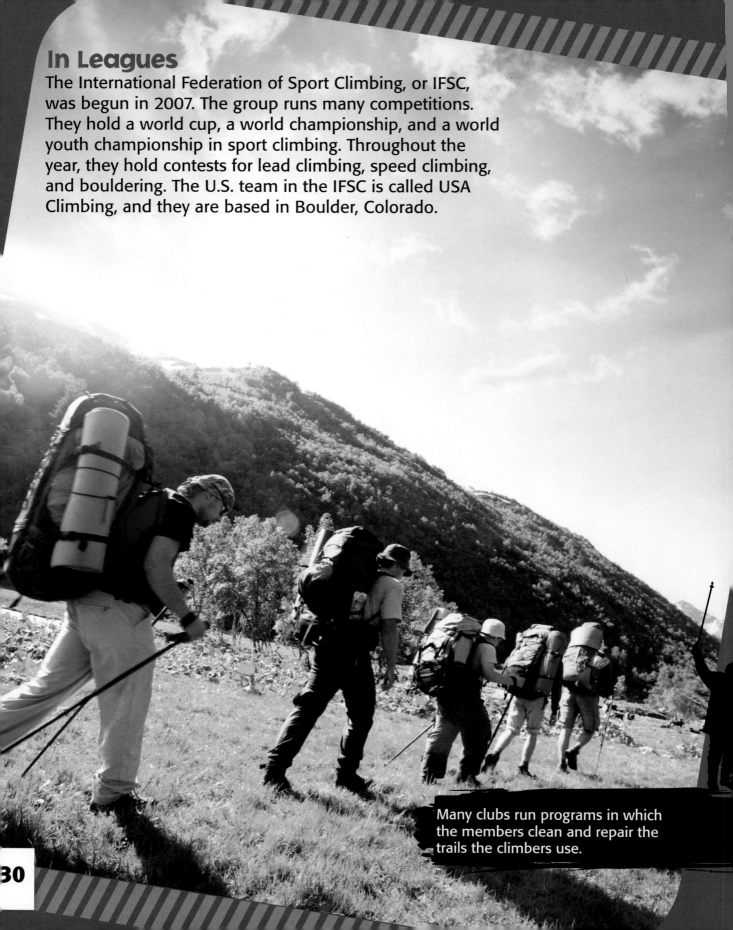

In Leagues

The International Federation of Sport Climbing, or IFSC, was begun in 2007. The group runs many competitions. They hold a world cup, a world championship, and a world youth championship in sport climbing. Throughout the year, they hold contests for lead climbing, speed climbing, and bouldering. The U.S. team in the IFSC is called USA Climbing, and they are based in Boulder, Colorado.

Many clubs run programs in which the members clean and repair the trails the climbers use.

Joining the Club

Other kinds of groups are dedicated to climbing in other ways. In areas where rock climbing and mountain climbing are local sports, local clubs help climbers meet one another. They create events where people can share skills.

On a national level, the American Alpine Club works to make sure that the sport is viewed favorably by people from the outside. Many of the mountains that mountaineers want to climb are in parks that are owned by the public. Leaders among the mountaineers work to keep the mountains open for climbing.

Some clubs allow members to check out gear similar to the way that people check out books at a library.

31

Rise to Fame

A university in Utah has started a competition that attracts hundreds of climbers. The participants see how fast they can get up a series of rocks, which are ranked by difficulty. The number of people who sign up for this yearly event has been growing. This is true of the entire sport of **competitive** climbing.

Inside Track

Today, there are thousands of indoor climbing walls where people can train. Schools with large fitness centers were among the first to build climbing walls. In addition, many sports clubs and other groups have invested in outdoor climbing structures.

A static move looks like a crawl.
A dynamic move is more like a hop.

TEST IT!

A climber can make **static moves**, forcing the body from one hold to the next and creating force to move forward bit by bit. The climber can also make a **dynamic move**. That is forcing the body upward with more energy at the start, almost like throwing the body forward. Static moves require less force overall, but more force over time. You can try both kinds of moves on the types of equipment found at a park.

AMONG THE STARS

The stars of mountain climbing are men and women who have explored new areas and broken records. Among them is Bern Goosen, an amazing South African who climbed Mount Kilimanjaro. He first reached Africa's tallest peak in 2003. This was more than a century after the first person climbed to the summit, but Goosen was breaking a different record. He was the first person to make it to the top in a wheelchair.

Mountains are used as a symbol for setting goals and meeting them.

First and Foremost

The hall of fame is filled with people who were the first to reach mountaintops, such as Reinhold Messner, the first person to reach the top of Mount Everest alone. These stars include Junko Tabei, the first woman to make it to the summit of Everest. Today's most famous mountaineers also include amazing **freestyle** climbers such as Alex Honnold. This extreme athlete is often pictured on rock walls, holding on by his fingers in a way that seems impossible. He holds a number of speed records.

Mount Kilimanjaro was formed by lava that began flowing a million years ago. In order to climb it, people often train first on Mount Meru, a smaller peak that is 45 miles away.

Selfless Acts

Among the legends of mountaineering are six climbers who saved the lives of five strangers on the North Ridge of Mount Everest. For their bravery, Tap Richards, Jason Tanguay, Dave Hahn, Andy Politz, Lobsang Temba Sherpa, and Phurba Tashi Sherpa have been honored. Members of the group won a special award, given by the American Alpine Club in celebration of the club's 100th year.

On high climbs, the climbers pause regularly to rest in camps. This helps their bodies get used to the thinning air. Failing to take steps like this is dangerous.

Call for Help

The climbers were on their way to the top of the mountain when they received a call for help. It came from a guide, a local man, who was with a climber who was sick with brain swelling. This is a dangerous condition that can happen when high in the mountains. While trying to reach the sick climber, the men came across three other climbers who had run out of oxygen. The team saved all five people, at great danger to themselves.

In the United States, a group called the Mountain Rescue Association trains people how to rescue climbers who need help.

EXTREME INTEREST

Can you see yourself climbing mountains? People who live near mountains are at an advantage. They can more easily find teachers and classes for the sport. But people anywhere can read or watch videos about mountaineering. Anyone can begin to build strength by hiking or doing other forms of exercise.

Class Act

A good way to start climbing is to join a fitness club with a rock wall. Now that indoor gyms offer safe spaces for people to learn, many young people are getting permission to climb for exercise. The rock walls feature safety ropes, and new climbers can get guidance to avoid a fall.

TEST IT!

A free fall is the state of falling through the air with **gravity** as the only force affecting you. Sky divers and BASE jumpers experience this. Because of gravity, a free-falling object accelerates, or speeds up. The increasing speed seems to add weight to the object. To see if you can feel the difference, let a partner drop a baseball into your cupped hands from just above. Then, have your partner drop the same ball into your hands from the top of a tall stoop, a slide, or some other safe platform.

Many people concentrate on the climb up, but the climb down can be especially dangerous.

Reach for the Sky

What do you see when you look at mountains? The history of mountaineering is filled with heroes who saw the challenge of climbing into the clouds. Learning about these climbers and their climbs is a way to appreciate the many possibilities in life. The stories of their courage help others see what happens when people set their minds on their goals.

By doing what makes them happy, mountaineers also help people recognize the majesty of Earth.

Exercise Rocks

Are you ready to follow in the climbing tradition? You can begin to prepare by hiking outdoors at every opportunity. You can start by climbing hills and stairways to build your strength. Climbing gives the body a super workout. It exercises muscles in the hands, arms, legs, chest, and back. The lungs and heart grow stronger, too.

Why not get going and see how far you can go?

When you feel fit, it is as if you can move mountains.

41

WORDS FOR IT

In daily life, when people are chipping in, they are helping to pay for something, such as a gift. In climbing, "chipping" is what climbers do when they make or change the "holds" on a mountainside. The holds are hand and foot supports, not delays of some kind. A grade in school is a mark a student receives for a project or a time period. But a "grade" in mountaineering is a measure of how hard it is to climb something.

You Don't Say

Mountain climbers have special words to talk about climbing, and often the same words mean something else in everyday life. For example, when a mountaineer is "wired," he or she knows a set of movements so well that it is easy to do. A "snot" is an extremely small hold found on an indoor wall.

Words in Context

Can you guess the meaning of these climbing words and phrases?

1. That old bolt is *manky*, so let's go the other way.

   manky: worthless

2. When I heard those rocks fall, I felt *gripped*.

   gripped: tired and scared

3. Look out! Halfway up, that rock has a real *cheese grater*.

   cheese grater: crack that can shred hands; also, a fall that shreds skin on knees and elsewhere

LEGENDS OF MOUNTAINEERING

The legends of mountaineering are men and women whose skills and daring won attention and awards. Among these legends are some news-making teens. Here are a few of the record breakers.

Five Famous Mountaineers

Barbara Washburn was the first woman to climb Mount McKinley, which is also known as Denali. She reached the top of North America's highest peak in 1947.

In 1963, **Jim Whittaker** was the first American to reach the summit of Mount Everest.

In 1984, **Lou Whittaker** led the first American ascent of Everest along the pass called the North Col. Lou is Jim Whittaker's twin.

Richard Bass was the first person to reach the top of all Seven Summits. He completed this goal in 1985.

In 2007, **Samantha Larson** became the youngest person to complete the Seven Summits, at age 18. In late 2011, she lost that title to Jordan Romero, a California climber. But she and her father, David Larson, remain the first father-daughter team to have climbed all seven.

Behind the Legends

The Seven Summits are Everest, Aconcagua, Denali (Mount McKinley), Kilimanjaro, Elbrus, Vinson Massif, and either Puncak Jaya (Carstensz Pyramid) or Kosciuszko. People do not agree on which of the last two peaks counts, so some people climb them both.

name	country	height	mountain range
Everest	Nepal	29,035 feet (8,850 m)	Himalaya
Aconcagua	Argentina	22,841 feet (6,962 m)	Andes
Denali	United States	20,320 feet (6,194 m)	Alaska Range
Kilimanjaro	Tanzania	19,340 feet (5,895 m)	Not part of a range
Elbrus	Russia	18,510 feet (5,642 m)	Caucasus Mountains
Vinson Massif	N/A	16,050 feet (4,892 m)	Ellsworth Mountains
Puncak Jaya (Carstensz Pyramid)	Indonesia	16,024 feet (4,884 m)	Sudirman Range
Kosciuszko	Australia	7,310 feet (2,228 m)	Great Dividing Range

American Mountaineers

There are a mountain of interesting facts about mountaineers. The list that follows shows just 18 of many Americans on the Seven Summits list, including some of the youngest people to have joined the club. You can use your library, and the Internet, to research these people and many others. Find out where they live or lived. Learn interesting facts about their lives, including any records that they hold. When did they reach the last summit? How old were they?

Caroline LeClaire	Glenn Porzak	Myung-Joon Kim
Chris Kopczynski	Hall Wendel	Paul Morrow
David Keaton	John Collinson	Robert Scull
Doug Mantle	John Dufficy	Samantha Larson
Geoff Tabin	Jordan Romero	Sandy Hill
Gerry Roach	Mary Lefever	Todd Burleson

Glossary

altitudes: heights; the measurement of space above a surface

back steps: steps using the outside edge of the front of the shoe, rather than the toe, heel, or inside edge

base camp: main camp for supplies, communication, and shelter

belayer: person who secures rope during climb

carbohydrates: components of food that supply energy

competitive: of or involving a test of skill

crampons: spikes placed on footwear to dig into snow or ice

dynamic move: movement in which the body is thrown into motion to help make progress

freestyle: allowing any trick or move from a somewhat standard set of tricks or moves

gravity: attraction between objects that have mass

hazards: sources of danger

hydrated: supported with enough water for health

qualifications: acts that determine if something is suitable, such as rounds in a competition

range: full measure covered or all possible values available

slope: a surface with one end higher than the other

static moves: motions in which the body movements are controlled and somewhat slow

techniques: a way of carrying out a given task

tension: the act of being stretched

thermal: using or producing heat

For More Information

Books

Borgenicht, David, and Bill Doyle. *Everest: You Decide How To Survive!* San Francisco, CA: Chronicle Books, 2011.

Hodge, Susie. *Mountain Survival.* Milwaukee, WI: Gareth Stevens, 2008.

Jenkins, Steve. *The Top of the World: Climbing Mount Everest.* Boston, MA: Houghton Mifflin, 1999.

Thomas, William David. *Mountain Rescuer.* Pleasantville, NY: Gareth Stevens, 2009.

Websites

The 7 Summits
7summits.com
The 7 Summits is a company that offers climbing expeditions, and its site is filled with related resources, including facts about the Seven Summits climbers.

Climbing Magazine
www.climbing.com
Climbing Magazine offers an online look at mountaineers in action. The site includes a selection of climbing videos.

National Geographic Education
education.nationalgeographic.com/education/st/?ar_a=4
The student section of this National Geographic site has a package of world study tools. To read about mountains, enter "mountains" in the search box.

Index